NEIL FINN

LYRICS

1978 – 2001

LOVE THIS LIFE

ALLEN&UNWIN

Allen & Unwin
83 Alexander Street
Crows Nest NSW 2065
Australia
Phone (61 2) 8425 0100
Fax: (61 2) 9906 2218
Email: info@allenandunwin.com
Web: www.allenandunwin.com

National Library of Australia
Cataloguing-in-Publication entry:

Finn, Neil.
Love this life: lyrics 1978–2001.

ISBN 1 86508 508 1.

1. Rock music—Texts. 2. Popular music—Texts. I. Title.

782.421660268.

Set in 12.25/14.25 Mrs Eaves by Midland Typesetters
Printed by Australian Print Group, Maryborough

10 9 8 7 6 5 4 3 2 1

CONTENTS

Foreword

It took me a good while to come around to the idea of a lyric book when it was suggested. A good lyric is always embedded in a good tune, the sound of the words and the rhythm and phrasing all seem to be integral and essential. On paper they may still have resonance but will usually not make the grade as good poetry. (There are some, I fear, that don't even make the grade as good lyrics.) I suppose I eventually warmed to the idea after gazing back over all my songs and sensing that there was an atmosphere and some distinct style which has emerged over the years for which I can feel some affection and pride.

As a teenager, I was the kind of listener that always latched on to a key line or two then made up my own impression of the song's meaning. As a songwriter, I found that the best way for me to come up with these key lines was to let myself drift off rudderless with my guitar and my voice, relying on accidental phrases popping out where the sound of the words was as important as their meaning. This approach has often delivered up quite potent images and, sometimes years later, I recognise layers of meaning that didn't immediately spring to mind. I have learned to trust this process, it seems right for me and I have always been happy to accept the occasional dig about 'not making sense'. I liken it to the kind of thought process that happens just before you go to sleep, where domestic and otherworldly images get muddled up with strange echoes and buried feelings.

I don't hold these lyrics as poetry, but among them are sentiments and ideas in which people have found comfort, empathy and inspiration. I feel truly blessed and grateful for this magical exchange.

Neil Finn

ONE NIL

THE CLIMBER

N. FINN

Beside me now are strangers to my eyes
They might be getting crazy might be wise
We're stranded either way
In such a lonely place
I'm looking out for you
Among the flies that wait in line for days on end
And nights so cold and always so intense
I try to reach the top most every day
In hope I turn my face up to the sky
The cover hangs so low
I see no sign of life
Nothing springs to mind
Among the flies that wait in line
For days on end and nights so cold
It's always so intense
And here we are
There's a smile between us and it's going on
You and me have always gotten through
Anyone can tell you that it's true
You feel it every time you drive away from home
The headlights hypnotise and they take you off towards
　　the sea
Into the night you run away with thoughts you cannot
　　hide
Vacant eyes can't describe my hunger
For your billowing arms
Mother I can't help thinking of you
Take this dull ache away

Rest Of The Day Off

N. FINN / W. MELVOIN / T. BLAKE

Totally wired and the game is up
I'm under the table
You carry my heart in the palm of your hand
As the clouds roll in, the party was rained out
Open up to find a man made home
And by four o'clock when the sun came out
We were beside ourselves
Taking the rest of the day off
Lying out the back
Slung in a hammock
Gathering reams of space and time

Two eyes that surrender
The call might come
Fire my anger and spoil the whole thing
It's not much fun when the pressure's on
And your luck has gone
But you squeeze my hand
We're taking the rest of the day off
We like to climb the rock
Before we have lunch
And we'll turn our backs on the whole damn bunch

You find the answer walking the dog
Down the south of Piha, it's over and done
Not a lot to say when the man calls up
The line goes dead and you're yesterday's news
I couldn't care less now I'm here with you
We're the only ones left and we're flat on our backs

Taking the rest of the day off
And you find it don't add up to much
When you're wrapped in a blanket of stars
With the one you love
Like two shiny dogs
With the one you love

Hole In The Ice

N. FINN / L. COLEMAN

Take it down, mess it up
Light a match, make a fire
Walk away as the money burns
It might just save your life
I play the happenstance
I see my fortune fly
Every time you lift the cup
And another long day goes by

And I won't travel into the straw daylight desire
I wrote that, some Eskimo gave me the line

Sit back and watch the money burn
Five days in a hot house hell
Once you're gone there's no return
And they're never gonna let you lie
I want my love to burn
Hotter than a comet's tail
I want my bed to cry
And I never wanna let you down

And I won't travel into the straw daylight desire
I wrote that, some Eskimo gave me the line

And all I ever do is therapy one on one, one on one
And you and I we might want the same thing one on
    one, one on one
I don't want a teacher to remind me, one on one, one
    on one
How to get something better out of my life

I play the happenstance
I see my fortune fly
Every time I lift the cup
And another long day goes by

And I won't travel into the pale moonlight desire
I wrote that, some Eskimo gave me the line
Your freedom is so precious that it makes me hurt
I learnt that, my teacher was my loneliness
And wisdom can be passed on by the one who's left
And freedom is so precious that it makes it work

WHEREVER YOU ARE

N. FINN

Wherever you are
It's 3 a.m. and I'm awake
Imagine the light
Upon your blue transparent face
Through coloured glass
It filters down to warmest red
Faded ...
I'm the one who reads your mind
See my life in your design
True companion at your side
You're gracious and good
When all around is turning bad
Restless and brave
When laid upon suburban grass
Your timing is right
Remove the sad persistent thought
Hold the course
I'm the one who reads your mind
Sees my life in your design
True companion at your side
I'll give you something
For when I'm not around
To make you smile
And if you think it then it must be true
If only I could make it through
Climb into my bed
Wherever you are
Wherever you are

Your timing is good
Remove the sad persistent thought
Hold the course
I'm the one who reads your mind
Sees my life in your design
True companion at your side
I'll leave you something for when I'm not around
To make you smile
Outside that wasteland
And if only I could make it through
If you think it then it must be true
Wherever you are

Last To Know

N. FINN / W. MELVOIN

Way down the track, made the wrong turn
Finished up where I started
You noticed a change come over me
Fell in love with my own reflection yeah
How does it feel beneath your own wheel
Feels like an accident waking up
Under a bus with my fingers crossed
Now is the time we could make it up
So you lost the fear it wasn't that bad
Left to your own devices yeah
Still a young girl eyes on the clock
Tick like a motor running out
Magnets and words up on the fridge
Speak to the poet in all of us
I missed the page that you thought about
Drew in the frost on the windowpane
But who I wonder could fail to notice
The aching silence came down
I'm humble now
I hope you might come back
In your own time
Left to your own devices
And so, that's how it goes
Never the first
Always the last to know

DON'T ASK WHY

N. FINN / W. MELVOIN

I never been to heaven but it feels alright
And I woke up this morning with a permanent smile
I walk in through your door
Hit the lights and get ready
As we hit the floor let our fingers do the walking
And the yellow pages will be flying through the sky

Maybe someone shook her leg
On a sailboat south of China
But you don't ask why
Got my picture on your mirror
Got my number on your notice board
And you don't ask why
Got my heart where I want it
Breathing heavy on her sinker lips
And you don't ask why
Sometimes life is getting better
And it happens on its own
It's beyond my control

Don't get too fast don't get too slow
You're messing with the beat like a samba meets a salsa
    baby
Error gorilla know what I mean
You get the biggest effect from the smallest machine
Who's that playing like Krupa on her fingertips
And you don't ask why
Got my picture on your mirror
Got my number on your notice board

And you don't ask why
Got my heart where I want it breathing heavy on her
    sinker lips
And you don't ask why
Somehow life is getting better
And it happens on its own
Where does love come from I don't know
So come on baby you're the chosen one
You know exactly what I need
You know exactly when the time has come
Here we go again

SECRET GOD

N. FINN / W. MELVOIN

Let's go climb up on the roof
In the twilight 360 degree view
As we lie down
Watch the fading light turn into stars
There you are
Secret god
Breathe my name
Secret god stir up the dust
Whisper my name
This reminds me of another place
Lonesome wolf comes down from the hills
And he's walking in circles howling at the moon
In another life he will be enchanted by a woman
Secret god stir up the dust
Breathe my name
Secret god stir up the dust
Whisper my name
I see a man collapse
In the doorway of a restaurant
And I'm holding my hand out
The first one there to help him up
Secret god stir up the dust
Whisper my name
Secret god stir up the dust
Breathe my name
Tine at hand stir up the dust
Breathe my name
Secret god whisper my name

Turn And Run

N. FINN

There's a light overhead, overhead
In the sky overhead, overhead
And I'm with you now in body and music and mind
And we're silent and still
Everything's so out of control tonight
In a plane that's flying fast
At a speed that makes me cry
Have you left me now
To trouble that won't let me lie
I'm awake all the time
You know where I stand
Holding my plastic gun
So turn and run
You cold killers of innocence
Against us there's no defence
Your flash and your wickedness
You can't break our love
Tie my hands behind my back
Put a gag on top of my mouth
But I won't give you up
Till silverware's covered in dust
And my shoes fall apart
And the tumbleweed runs
Over my desert heart
So turn and run
You cold killers of innocence
Against us there's no defence

Your flash and your wickedness
Will surely bring you down again
Somehow we must stay afloat
Won't give in to the undertow
Some things you will never know
You can't break our love
You can pull us down
But you can't break our love

ELASTIC HEART

N. FINN

Spring back elastic heart
We are not angry now
Somehow we both dissolve
All our weight is gone
And tenderness
Is ours again
Can we forget the past
Find us an open road
Picture the two of us
Window caravan
Silhouette against the sky
As we spin around with our arms entwined
Delirious
In love
Spring back elastic heart
We are not angry now
Picture the two of us
With our arms entwined
We should be thankful then
For our disgrace
Delirious in love

ANYTIME

N. FINN

I see a dog upon the road
Running hard to catch a cat
My car is pulling to a halt
The truck behind me doesn't know
Everything is in the balance
Of a moment I can't control
And your sympathetic strings
Are like the stirrings in my soul

I could go at anytime
There's nothing safe about this life
I could go at anytime

Find the meaning of the act
Remember how it goes
Every time you take the water
And you swim against the flow
The world is all around us
The days are flying past
And fear is so contagious

But I'm not afraid to laugh
I could go at anytime
There's nothing safe about this life
I could go at anytime

Anytime (come without warning)
Anytime (it could be so easy)
A walk in the park (or maybe when I'm sleeping)
Anytime (see the clouds come over)

Rain or shine (I make you so unhappy)
Let's make it right

I feel like I'm in love
With a stranger I'll never know
Although you're still a mystery I'm so glad I'm not
    alone

I could go at anytime
There's nothing safe about this life
Make it so easy to fly in the night
I could go at anytime
I could go at anytime

DRIVING ME MAD

N. FINN

Deadlines again
Feel like hiding out
No sign of comfort yet
Have a nap while no one's looking
Bring some inspiration to the man
In my head
A namesake out of reach
Strange days upon us now
We leave the dust of conversation
Hanging in the light above the bed
Leave me now
Cos tonight it's driving me mad
I guess I'll be all right
But tonight it's driving me mad
Year after year
Demons always come
Fail to materialise
Way beyond my understanding
Find my only comfort in your hands
Hold me now
Cos tonight it's driving me mad
This dream can fill you up
But tonight it's driving me mad

Hey diamond girl
Restless in my head
Say what lies between us
A host of everyday distractions
But most of all it's music taking me

It's driving me mad
Still I can't refuse
Even when it's driving me mad
I guess I'll be all right
When tomorrow brings some relief
This dream can fill you up
So put it out and find what's underneath

INTO THE SUNSET

N. FINN

Here lies a place
Won't let me languish
Hears all my footsteps and waits
Watch how she fades into the sunset
A vision spectacular in grace
Hunger for the world travel
Stimulating discussion lift me
Faster into the weakness
Off the wall into blackness
Gifted
Red eyes reflect
Open the suitcase
Spread all your clothes on the floor
Much like it was
Ten years ago
Time on the clock
Don't want to waste it
Watch how she fades into the sunset
A vision spectacular in grace
Hunger for the world travel
Stimulating discussion lift me

Faster into the weakness
Off the wall into blackness
Gifted
And I'm away from home
And it's a way of life
And I'm flying high
And I'm a wheeling gull

Here now I come to rest
Under a lion rock
Over marine parade
Maybe this time
Here I'll stay

AFTER GLOW

I Am In Love

N. FINN

Called out to prove my love
You reply by getting defensive
Called out to prove my love
Now you should be able to sense it
I am full of your dreams
I let you sleep with the lights on
Stay with me might as well
Be the kind of girl you want to be

I am in love
I am in love
I am a fool
Fell from above

These things that I have done
They would be a test of anyone
How am I meant to see
You dressed up like your mother
They say marry your father
I hope that don't reflect on me
They say marry your mother
I hope that don't put you in her company

I am in love
I am in love
I am a fool
There is no other
I am in love
I am in love

And what I say is no lie
But it's enough to make you wonder
And I'm the one that you want to trust
And I am the one that you want to trample
In the dust

I am in love
I am in love
I am a fool
There is no other
I am in love
I am in love

SACRED COW

N. FINN

Deliberate provocation
It's what you gave to me
You got me going
You got me going

How could such a simple thing
Get so out of control
You let me down again
You let me down again

I know my place inside your heart
A painted figure that glows in the dark
No, you're not mysterious now
I don't worship that sacred cow

Am I here
Am I here
Am I here yet
You'd never know it
You'd never know it

Went home in a jealous rage
You were rolling on the grass
In a younger age
You know what's good for me
I know you're too good for me

Cause I have seen inside your heart
Religious figures that glow in the dark
No, you're not too precious now
And I don't worship that scared cow

Go try as you may
You'll get a short shift on judgement day

You let me down again
You let me down again
And I know my place inside your heart
Painted figure that glows in the dark
No, you're not too precious now
And I don't worship that scared cow

Go, try as you may, you'll get a short shift on
    judgement day

You Can Touch

N. FINN

It could spell my near defeat
You could find it's what you need
And tears will fall and oceans will rise
I feel the fear and I know I'm alive
And you can touch me I won't hide
You can touch me I won't die

My condition is hard to define
I'm thin and pale and I need to unwind
I see no future from where I stand
For the present I am in your hand
And you can touch me I won't hide
You can touch me I won't die

And tears will fall and oceans will rise
I feel the fear and I know I'm alive
We're only passing through
And you can touch me I won't hide
You can touch me I won't die
You can touch me I won't die

I Love You Dawn

N. FINN

I love you dawn
You understand
The strength of ten men in your hands
It was another tear it was another time
All is not lost
And we will shine
Beneath the tall trees I believe
There is nothing you and me can't do together if we try
The day is long and the nights are cold just a song to
    warm your soul
I don't want to see you cry

I love you dawn
You understand
The strength of ten men in your hands
Was another tear was another time
All is not lost and we will shine
Above the billboard and the hoards
Magazines and rock awards
We can afford to pay our bills
The day is long and the nights are cold
Just a song to warm your soul
I don't want to see you cry
I love you dawn

I love you dawn
You understand
The strength of ten men in your hands
Was another tear, another year, another time

All is not lost and we will shine
Shine shine

Dr Livingston
N. FINN

Steam ship sail down the river
Fight the mosquitoes that lie in the swamp
White smoke cover the jungle see Dr Livingston land
    with a thump

Down where the sad willows gather
Young women weep for their dying babies
I am a white man in Africa
If I were to stay here there'd be no one to save me
I hear the drums, I know it's urgent
I hear survival in his hands
Switch to record, I get the picture
But I will never understand

Mad world invisible army
Blow up the bridges and come like a storm
Young girl eyes full of promise
Carry the baby and keeping it warm
Down where the sad willows gather
Young men go down on their knees
I am a white man in Africa
With more than just my god to appease

I hear the drums, I know it's urgent
I hear survival in his hands
Switch to record I get the picture
But I will never understand

How there is love in his face
In the midst of all this waste

In the Mozambique sun under the gun
I hear the drums, I hear survival in his hands, I hear
the drums
There is a curse upon this land
Hear the drums, know it's urgent
Hear survival in his hands
Hit record, get the picture, I will never understand

LESTER

N. FINN

Saw my life go flashing past
In the eyes of a faithful friend
Four legs for life
And the screeching tyres never seem to end
I will change if Lester lives
Not mess him round just cause I own him
He was nearly wiped away
But he had good luck and strong bones
You make me clench my teeth
Us humans ain't got dignity
Eat my plants and steal my things
But you're the head of security
I will change if Lester lives
Not mess him round just cause I own him
He was nearly wiped away
But he had good luck and strong bones
Inside and behind him
I will change if Lester lives
Not mess him round
Just cause I own him

Anyone Can Tell

N. FINN

I dream of a place that's hedged with roses
Where the man in the middle don't talk in riddles
You get hung on every single word
Some call it high some call it low
When they hear about things they don't want to know
But the truth is still a valuable thing
Don't get caught with your pants down baby
In this world the criminals sing
There is another world waiting
Anyone can tell
Anyone can tell
Anyone can tell that I'm not lying
You can hide your face, pull it into shapes
But you can't escape the lie forever
I dream of a place that's overrun by children
And the lord is in the kitchen
You do your work and you get your rewards
Cause what you are is all that really matters
What is left you can easily scatter
On the ground ahead covered in mud
Don't step on my principles baby
In spite of what you have done
One day you will have the wisdom
I will tell you everything's great
Anyone can tell that I'm not lying
You can hide your face
You can change your shape
But you can't escape the lie forever

Anyone can tell
Anyone can tell

RECURRING DREAM

N. FINN

Within myself there are a million things
Spilling over, falling out into a silent stream

Feel the warm wind touch me
Hear the waters crashing
See my windows wiping clean
It's my recurring dream

Within myself a secret world returns
Over and over, where the white flame of desire burns

Feel the warm wind touch me
Hear the waters crashing
See my windows wiping clean
It's my recurring dream

LEFT HAND

N. FINN

It was typical of you
To give it to me plain
The sign on your door
Said make your mind up or go away
It was difficult for me to single you out
Left hand wants to know what the right is doing
Whichever way we miss out on something
We're free but there is one thing
We're not facing
It was typical of you to feather your nest
I try to explain but me and my big mouth
Were laid to rest
There's nowhere to go
I'm not hanging around
Left hand
Pick me up then you put me down, put me down
Left hand wants to know what the right is doing
Whichever way we miss out on something
We're free there is something we're not facing, no, left
    hand, left hand
Wants to know what the right is doing

Time Immemorial

N. FINN

Start in the way that you want to go on
Tear down the fence that you sit upon
It was good while it lasted but now it has gone
So face up to what you have done
For time immemorial, time immemorial, time
A glorious contest to find the invincible one

And I will know everything there is
Goodbye to you and your money
And I will go anywhere you say if you take away all the
    cameras
The house that we live in is falling apart
There's no guarantee cause we got it for free
And all the pretenders to somebody's throne
Are finding it out on their own
For time immemorial, time immemorial, time
Will go on a mission to find the invincible one

And I will know everything there is
Goodbye to you and your public
And I will go everywhere you say if you don't charge
    admission
Okay we're lucky but then again

Time immemorial, time immemorial, time
Will go on a mission to find the invincible one

And I will know everything there is
Goodbye to you and your money
And I will go anywhere you say

Sell me the show, the secrets of your house
And I will know everything you say
Take away all the cameras, the cameras
And I will go anywhere you say
If you don't charge admission, admission

TRY WHISTLING THIS

Last One Standing

N. FINN

Hand me down my favourite coat
Show what you're made of, surprise us both
Fly in the night, slow down town
Brake too fast, bring us round, bring us round

And our finest days have come
Summer nights go on so long
So high I might as well be gone

And you are magnificent
I can see you with my eyes closed
You're the last one standing

Lean and hungry with a fire in your eyes
I'll play catch up, you can show me where it's at
I'll go along with anything that you want to do
Everyday I'm making ground
So high I might as well be gone

And you are magnificent
I can see you with my eyes closed
When you come walking into my house
I'll be the last one standing

If you want you can get there
Night vision and I find your white doves
Landing in your treasure towers
And I promise that I won't look back
Everyday we're making ground
So high I might as well be gone

And you are magnificent
I can see you with my eyes closed
When you come walking into my house
I'll be the last one standing

Souvenir

N. FINN

Don't ask the question
You won't like the answer
Get up off your chair
There's nothing for you here
Where the guests like souvenirs
They play with you till you're all worn out
Back where the guests like souvenirs

Prison colour blue
It's a uniform of choice
Count yourself lucky
That you don't write the software
And the guests like souvenirs
They play with you till you're all worn out
Back where the guests take photographs
They hope you had a good night

Loosen up your tie
Make the viewers cry
I cannot pretend to cry

Memorise by heart
Every single part
There's nothing for you here
Where the guests like souvenirs
They play with you till you're all worn out
Back where the guests like souvenirs
They hope you had a good night

Each night I fall
Right off the stage
No one's impressed

KING TIDE

N. FINN

It's a dark and empty room
The sun beating hard on your door
Feel emotion roar within you
You're flesh and blood like anyone

Make some sense of your life
Move your hand and make the mark
I don't know why you're so confused
You're flesh and blood, there's no excuse

And the hunger inside
Won't go away it's starting to rise
And the longer you hide
The more you deny
And the sea rushes in

The wind is howling at your back
The past is always overturned
It's a dead man who would refuse
And twice the man to fill his shoes

And the hunger inside
Won't go away it's starting to rise
And the longer you hide
The more you deny
And the hunger inside
Won't go away it's starting to rise
And the sea rushes in
Into my world

I can feel the king tide coming
All my senses overflowing
One man waiting out the back
Horns blow and cymbals crash
So paint a circle in the sky
We are breathless in the arms of love
There's a bruise on my back
And a new understanding too

Try Whistling This

N. FINN / J. MOGINIE

Tales from my head
You can't buy the book
No one's listening
But I guess you could
Try whistling this

You say you're tired
Liquid as water
But you'll succumb now
As I stroke your back
Cause I'm the best that you know

And every time you think of me
I hope you think of true romance
And every time you want to leave
You give us both another chance

Warmest welcome
Violent stranger
Well he said come here
As you pushed me down
Impossible to do

In high heels
Walking into walls
Do you ever wonder
If you're here at all
Try whistling this

And my words are ringing in my ear
Drawing your attention out to all the things that you
ignore
And if I can't be with you I would rather have a
different face
And if I can't be near you I would rather be adrift in
space
And if the gods desert us I would burn this chapel into
flames
And if someone tries to hurt you I would put myself in
your place

SHE WILL HAVE HER WAY

N. FINN

I might be old but I'm someone new she said
I'm so sore that I could cry always
In the night lay your tired arms
She will have her way
Somehow I will still believe her
It's the life I've been frightened of she said
Deathly silence and especially the dark
Feels like I am heavy and my spirit has died
She will have her way
Somehow I will still believe her
She will have her way
One day I will come back
Still no end in sight
Though I travel far and wide
A dying man is doing time
Thinker, soldier terrified
And she will have her way
Somehow I will still believe her
She will have her way
One day I will come back

SINNER

N. FINN

See it anyone, got my eyes got my face
Sing it everyone, got my nose got my blood
Conscience plays upon me now
Safe until my luck runs out
Cuckoos call, pendulum swings
I thought you knew everything
Lift my hands make the cross

Sinner I have never learned
Beginner I cannot return
Forever I must walk this earth
Like some forgotten soldier

These things I should keep to myself
But I feel somehow strangely compelled
Under moonlight I stood wild and naked
Felt no shame just my spirit awakened
Sinner, got my eyes got my face
Fireball drop from the sky
All my dreams have come to pass
Where's my faith is it lost
Can't see it till you cast it off

Sinner there is no such thing
Beginner I have learned to sing
Forever I must walk this earth
Like some forgotten soldier
Today I am still disconnected
To the face that I saw in the clouds
And the closest I get to contentment
Is when all of the barriers come down

Twisty Bass

N. FINN

The hangman's in the noose
The prisoner is loose
The wheel has come around
And the velvet curtain coming down

And I left it there
The suitcase on a chair
I feel my weight
And something tellls me
There's a river underground
In a place where there's no one to be found

And no one came to see
The oldest show in town

Santa's on the cross
And innocence is lost
The music's in your mind
And the windscreen wipers move in time

No one came to see
The oldest show in town
And the stranger was a ghost
The killer was a priest
Took the first excuse
Made the madness seem cute lipped
On your own you'll find there's no escape
There are many ways to choose
And I don't know which one you should take

A home is all you want
On the back of a truck driving down the street
It doesn't seem so much
But it's all you need to make your life complete

And no one came to see
The oldest show in town

I lean the slightest bit towards you
White turns into brown, light goes to black
Your eyes danced in my reflection
And the horse ate my trousers

Loose Tongue

N. FINN

Remember my loose tongue
Forget what I just said
I'd crawl over broken glass
If we could start again
Before our plans were made
When the world was young
The house is falling down
Because of my loose tongue

Shouldn't say so much
Shouldn't talk so loud
No sooner on your lips
Than it's all over town
In all our given days
How many gone to waste
A good man has been hung
Because of my loose tongue

Your skin is changing its hue
Your guard is coming down fast
Looks like someone I knew
Uncovered happiness at last

All the wagging tongues
Too much information
In the future now
Under massive doubt
The papers on the street
Get trampled under feet

And they settled for a princely sum
Goodwill is coming down
And when it rains
Your well is full

He's only halfway through his life
He's only used up all his time

TRUTH

N. FINN

Remember who we are
Supple and new
If I lose my way
Tell me the truth for all it's worth
Lifting up your head
Show me my rescue

What I said
Truth is worth more than pride
Truth is worth more than pride

Everything you do
Continues long after you've gone
Circle overhead the view from the bed
So high and lonely
Sixteen times a day
He comes to ground to get some attention

What I said
Truth is worth more than pride
Truth it's worth more than pride
Truth it's worth more than pride

They have showered me with riches
And they say that I am worthy
Of their love and their attention
But they still don't know the
Truth

Everything you do
Continues long after you've gone

What I said
It's worth more than pride
Truth is worth more than pride
Truth can not be denied

ASTRO

N. FINN

You weightless astronaut
You sunset diving bird
A cool wind set upon
The branches of a tree

You holding my attention
You are my first impression
And I can recognise
The life that I've been given

One day they will discover you
Low cloud moving cross the sky
One day they will uncover you
Young girl wash the sleep out of your eye

Dust on my piano
Wool rest never sleeping
All your best one-liners
Borrowed from a film

The thing that gets to me is
How you'll never free him
How the spirit yearns
Your body is a prison

One day they will discover you
Low cloud moving cross the sky
One day they will uncover you

And the thing that gets to me
Is how you're never free

How the spirit yearns
Your body is a prison

Bright as her eyes
Wide in the night
Why can't you see me
Come with the wind
Time to begin
There'll be no compromise
When all you want is wrapped around you
There's no saints, preserve us when we're dying
To pick us up from where we're lying

One day they will discover you
One day they will uncover you
Bright as her eyes
Wide in the night
They will discover you
They will discover you

DREAM DATE
N. FINN

Remove yourself
From the past
Wherever you are
You don't have to stay

Old and wise
Lion's eyes
I wish you were here
To give me advice

Lightweight
Dream date
Fly or fall
It's my call

In the club
Halfway up
Whisky at five
A weekend retreat

Brave and young
The bells have rung
They're playing the tune
I'm tapping my feet

Lightweight
Dream date
Fly or fall
It's my call

Friend or foe
It's hard to know
I wish you were here
To give me advice

Lightweight
Dream date
Fly or fall
It's my call

Lightweight
Dream date
Fly or fall
It's my call

Faster Than Light

N. FINN

Close your eyes go to sleep
Close your eyes get so dizzy
World is spinning in your bed
I know where the sun goes
Gone to wake up the sparrows
In England it's morning

In time you'll see that some things
Travel faster than light
In time you'll recognise
That love is larger than life

Now you know what you're missing
Now you've seen that I'm willing
If you're looking for the message
Close your eyes
Do you hear what I'm thinking
Is it how you imagined

In time you'll see that some things
Travel faster than light
In time you'll recognise
That love is larger than life

And praise will come to those whose kindness
Leaves you without debt
And bends the shape of things
That haven't happened yet

Close your eyes

It comes changing like a lizard
Close your eyes

I know where the sun goes
I've seen the world turning

In time you'll find that some things
Travel faster than light
In time you'll recognise that
Love is larger than life

And praise will come to those whose kindness
Leaves you without debt
And bends the shape of things to come
That haven't happened yet

ADDICTED

N. FINN

Hear the words a jumble try this tongue twister
Kevin has a caterpillar squeezed between his fingers
Hear the mailman come let's see what he delivers

And you wait and it makes you feel strange
As if you were afraid
And you lie with a look to the side
And you say I was addicted to the drug
But now I know when I've had enough

I could curl up and sleep on the floor
But I'm riding the train a hundred miles an hour
It feels like this train might never stop ooh

Watching static on the television
When the morning comes
And you wait and it makes you feel strange
As if you were deranged
With a look to the side
And you say I was addicted to the drug
But now I know when I've had enough
So far, we've come so far

IDENTICAL TWIN

N. FINN

Beware late night thinking
Before starlight's over
The world has been shaken

Rain
I felt myself sinking
And you lay above me
Identical twin

Beware violent mood swing
Before I can stop it
The word has been spoken

Rain
I felt myself sinking
And you lay above me
The earth drew me in
Identical twin

Some say that's good
And you can be certain
You did all you could
Leave all your questions
I felt myself sinking
And you lay above me
My high flying one
My light fingered foe
My light field below

808 Song

N. FINN

I recognise the warning signs
But is it too much to expect
Do you remember who it was
It's a danger to forget

Not a whisper from my mouth
Radiate the circle around
Everything you touch is art
Guess I knew it from the start

Good will be mine
You can talk till your face don't shine
But your dreams will come clean
And violins will tremble
When you pass

With whose presence I was blessed
So much better in the flesh
You can try your very best
But it won't get you that far

Good will have mine
You can talk till your face don't shine
And your days will come clean
And violins will tremble
When you pass

TOKYO

N. FINN

He has a house that's well laid out
He has a dog that doesn't bark
And a lamp by Frank Lloyd Wright
I can hardly stand up
But I feel something going on in Tokyo
There is pain and pleasure to be sold
And at last I have a place to go
Alive in Tokyo
She has a soft and supple mouth
She has a wild and wicked grin
And she demands attention
I can hardly stand up
But I feel something going on in Tokyo
There is pain and pleasure to be sold
And the western devil has got your soul
But you don't know
What's going on in Tokyo
I have a tightness in my chin
I can't find a single word to say
I think I need to splash my face
I can hardly stand up
But I feel something going on in Tokyo
There is pain and pleasure to be sold
And at last I have a place to go
Alive in Tokyo

RECURRING DREAM

EVERYTHING IS GOOD FOR YOU
N. FINN

I see a man with a flag and he leads the procession
And a woman shedding tears for a man locked in
    prison
And the two locked eyes and for a moment I was taken
All paths lead to a single conclusion

Everything is good for you
If it doesn't kill you
Everything is good for you
One man's ending
Is another one's beginning
Everything is good for you

It's a nightmare jump into a restless ocean
Where the reckless come to state their position
And if you come undone it might just set you free

Everything is good for you
If it doesn't kill you
Everything is good for you
One man's ending
Is another one's beginning

Bring back your head
Here comes trouble
To turn the angry word
Cover you up

Everything is good for you
If it doesn't kill you

Everything is good for you
If it doesn't kill you
Everything is good for you
It is good for you

INSTINCT

N. FINN

I lit the match, I lit the match
I saw another monster turn to ash
Felt the burden lifting from my back
Do you recognise a nervous twitch
That exposes the weakness of the myth

When your turn comes around
And the light goes on
And you feel your attraction again
Your instinct can't be wrong

Separate the fiction from the fact
I've been a little slow to react
But it's nearly time to flick the switch
And I'm hanging from a single stitch
Laughing at the stony face of gloom

When your turn comes around
And the light goes on
And you feel your attraction again
Your instinct can't be wrong

Feelings come and go
And the true present lies are calling down
They're calling down
Laughing at the stony face of doom

When your turn comes around
And the days get long
And you feel your attraction to him
Your instinct can't be wrong

Not The Girl You Think You Are

N. FINN

You're not the girl you think you are, no no
They're not his shoes under your bed, yeah yeah
He'll take you places in his car
That you won't forget, no

And all the people that you know
Will turn their heads as you go by
But you'll be hard to recognise
With the top down and the wind blowing, blowing

He won't deceive you
He'll tell you the truth
Woman, he'll be no trouble
He won't write you letters
Full of excuses
Come on, I believe you have one in a million

You're not the girl you think you are
There's someone standing in your place
The bathroom mirror makes you look tall
But it's all in your head, in your head

He won't deceive you
Or tell you the truth
Woman, he'll be no trouble
He won't write you letters
Full of excuses
Come on, believe you have one in a million

He won't deceive you
Or tell you the truth
Come on, believe you have won
You're not the girl you think you are
Believe you have won
You're not the girl you think you are
Believe you have won
You're not the girl you think you are

FINN

Last Day Of June

N. FINN

The firelight plays on me
The choir ignites behind me
The rising voice of discontent
All the guardian angels
You can bang the drum
Look what we've become
I hope there might be one of us
Who calls the tune
Last day of June

The so called third dimension
Hardly deserves a mention
The first and second stages
Have been confused for ages
Knowledge has been lost
How much does it cost
I hope there might be one of us
Who calls the tune
Last day of June
Who breaks the news
Last day of June

The city draws its breath in
I can almost hear it thinking
There are people within my walls
See their wild disorder
Driving their machines
Swarming like a million bees
I hope there might be one of us

Who calls the tune
Last day of June
Who speaks the truth
Last day of June
Who breaks the news
Last day of June

Together Alone

Kare Kare

N. FINN

I was standing on a wave
Then I made the drop
I was lying in a cave
In the solid rock
I was feeling pretty brave
Till the lights went off

Sleep by no means comes too soon
In a valley lit by the moon

We left a little dust
On his Persian rug
We gathered up our clothes
Got the washing done
In a long-forgotten place
Who'll be the first to run?

Sleep by no means comes too soon
In a valley lit by the moon

I was floating on a wave
Then I made the drop
I was climbing up the walls
Waiting for the band to stop

You can say the magic words
I got my sensors on
And this is the only place
That I always run from

Sleep by no means comes too soon
In a valley lit by the moon

In My Command

N. FINN

We're standing in a deep dark hole
Beneath the sky as black as coal
It's just a fear of losing control
You know so well
Don't miss it when the moment comes
Be submissive just this once
Imagine there is something to be done
Some truth to tell

I would love
To trouble you in your time of need
Lose your way
It's a pleasure when you're in my command

Juggle like a diplomat
Struggle to hold on to your hat
Swinging like an acrobat
But time will tell
The clock is dripping on the wall
Listen to the rise and fall
Close your eyes and hear the call
You know so well

I would love
To trouble you in your time of need
Lose your way
It's a pleasure when you're in my command
Put on your wings
You're responsible for everything

Desolate in anger or safe in isolation
You're about to be the victim of a holy visitation
By the rights I have been given

Put on your wings
You're not responsible for anything
I would love
To trouble you in your time of need
Lose your way
It's a pleasure when you're in my command

Nails In My Feet

N. FINN

My life is a house
You crawl through the window
Slip across the floor and into the reception room
You enter the place
Of endless persuasion
Like a knock on the door when there's ten or more
    things to do

Who was that calling?
You my companion
Run to the water on a burning beach
It brings me relief

Pass through the walls
To find my intentions
Circle round in a strange hypnotic state
I look into space
There is no connection
A million points of light and a conversation I can't face

Cast me off one day
To lose my inhibitions
Sit like a lap-dog on a matron's knee
Wear the nails on your feet

I woke up the house
Stumbled in sideways
The lights went on and everybody screamed surprise
The savage review
It left me gasping
But it warms my heart to see that you can do it too

Total surrender
Your touch is so tender
Your skin is like water on a burning beach
And it brings me relief

In the back row, under the stars
And the ceiling is my floor

BLACK AND WHITE BOY

N. FINN

Black and white boy, black and white boy
You're so extreme, you're so confused
Colour me in, whatever mood I'm in
I could be still in touch with you

And you're full of the wonder of spring
It's all sweetness and light that you bring
And a room full of people will fall to your infinite
    charm
But when darkness should quickly descend
You go quietly my miserable friend
To the depths of despair you will crawl
Black and white boy

Black and white boy, black and white boy
You're so extreme, you're so confused
Colour me in, whatever mood I'm in
I could be still in touch with you

When you shake off the shadows of night
And your eyes are so clear and so bright
You make fools of the liars and creeps
Put a rose in my cheeks
But when demons have climbed on your back
You are vicious and quick to attack
And you put on a wonderful show
Do you really, really think I don't know?

Black and white boy, black and white boy
And you run like a cat to the cream

And you're acting so nice it's obscene
And you put on a wonderful show
Do you really, really think I don't know?
Black and white boy, black and white boy
Black and white boy, black and white boy

FINGERS OF LOVE

N. FINN

Can you imagine that
An itch too sensitive to scratch
The light that falls through the cracks
An insect too delicate to catch?
I hear the endless murmur
Every blade of grass that shivers in the breeze
And the sound, it comes to carry me
Across the land and over the sea

And I can't look up
Fingers of love move down
And I can't look back
Fingers of love move down

Colour is its own reward
Colour is its own reward
The chiming of a perfect chord
Let's go jumping overboard
Into waves of joy and clarity
Your hands come out to rescue me
And I'm playing in the shallow water
Laughing while the mad dog sleeps

And I can't look up
Fingers of love move down
And I won't be helped
Fingers of love move everywhere

And there is time yet
To fall by the way

From the cradle to the grave
From the palace to the gutter
Beneath the dying rays of the sun
Lie the fingers of love

Into waves of joy and clarity
A fallen angel walked on the sea
And I'm playing in the shallow water
Laughing while the mad dog sleeps

And I can't look up
Fingers of love move down
And I won't be helped
Fingers of love move everywhere

There is time yet
For you to find me
And all at once
Fingers of love move down

PINEAPPLE HEAD

N. FINN

Detective is flat, no longer is always flat out
Got the number of the getaway car
Didn't get very far

As lucid as hell and these images
Moving so fast like a fever
So close to the bone
I don't feel too well

And if you choose to take that path
I will play you like a shark
And I'll clutch at your heart
I'll come flying like a spark to inflame you

Sleeping alone for pleasure
The pineapple head, it spins and spins
Like a number I hold
Don't remember if she was my friend
It was a long time ago

And if you choose to take that path
I will play you like a shark
And I'll clutch at your heart
I'll come flying like a spark to inflame you

And if you choose to take that path
Would you come to make me pay?
I will play you like a shark
And I'll clutch at your heart
I'll come flying like a spark to inflame you

LOCKED OUT

N. FINN

I've been locked out
I've been locked in
But I always seem to come back again
When you're in that room
What do you do?
I know that I will have you in the end

And the clouds they are crying on you
And the birds are offering up their tunes
In a shack as remote as a mansion
You escape into a place where nothing moves

I've been locked out
And I know we're through
But I can't begin to face up to the truth
I waited so long for the walls to crack
But I know that I will one day have you back

And the hills are as soft as a pillow
And they cast a shadow on my bed
And the view when I look through my window
Is an altarpiece I'm praying to for the living and the
    dead

Twin valley shines in the morning sun
I send a message out to my only one

And I've been locked out and I know we're through
But I can't begin to face up to the truth
I waited so long for the walls to crack
But I know that I will one day have you back

And I work with the bees and the honey
And every night I circle like the moon
And it's a act of simple devotion
But it can take forever when you've got something to
    prove

I've been locked out

PRIVATE UNIVERSE

N. FINN

No time, no place to talk about the weather
The promise of love is hard to ignore
You said the chance wasn't getting any better
The labour of love is ours to endure

The highest branch on the apple tree
Was my favourite place to be
I could hear them breaking free
But they could not see me

I will run for shelter
Endless summer lift the curse
It feels like nothing matters
In our private universe

I have all I want, is that simple enough?
A whole lot more I'm thinking of
Every night about six o'clock
The birds come back to the palm to talk
They talk to me, birds talk to me
If I go down on my knees

I will run for shelter
Endless summer lift the curse
It feels like nothing matters
In our private universe
Feels like nothing matters
In our private universe

And it's a pleasure that I have known
And it's a treasure that I have gained
And it's a pleasure that I have known

It's a tight squeeze but I won't let go
Time is on the table and the dinner's cold

I will run for shelter
Endless summer lift the curse
It feels like nothing matters
In our private universe

Walking On The Spot

N. FINN

At odd times we slip
Slither down the dark hole
Fingers point from old windows
An eerie shadow falls
Walking on the spot
To show that I'm alive
Moving every bone in my body
From side to side

Will we be in our minds
When the dawn breaks?
Can we look the milkman in the eye?
The world is somehow different
You have all been changed
Before my very eyes

Walk around your home
And pour yourself a drink
Fire one more torpedo baby
Watch the kitchen sink
Lounging on the sofa maybe
See the living room die
Dishes are unwashed and broken
All you do is cry

Will we be in our minds
When the dawn breaks?
Can we look the milkman in the eye?
The world is somehow different

You have all been changed
Before my very eyes

Dishes are unwashed and broken
All you do is cry

DISTANT SUN

N. FINN

Tell me all the things you would change
I don't pretend to know what you want
When you come around and spin my top
Time and again, time and again
No fire where I lit my spark
I am not afraid of the dark
Where your words devour my heart
And put me to shame, put me to shame

And your seven worlds collide
Whenever I am by your side
And dust from a distant sun
Will shower over everyone

You're still so young to travel so far
Old enough to know who you are
Wise enough to carry the scars
Without any blame, there's no one to blame
It's easy to forget what you learned
Waiting for the thrill to return
Feeling your desire burn
You're drawn to the flame

When your seven worlds collide
Whenever I am by your side
And dust from a distant sun
Will shower over everyone
Dust from a distant sun
Will shower over everyone

And I'm lying on the table
Washed out in the flood
Like a Christian fearing vengeance from above
I don't pretend to know what you want
But I offer love

Seven worlds collide
Whenever I am by your side
And dust from a distant sun
Will shower over everyone

As time slips by, and on and on

CATHERINE WHEELS
N. FINN

No night to stay in
Bad moon is rising again
Dice rolls, you burn
Come down, I fear
As that cold wheel turns
I know what I know
Sad Claude's been sleeping around
To stroke the right nerve
Whose needs do I serve
As Catherine's wheel turns?

She was always the first to say gone
She's got her Catherine wheels on
Always the first to say gone
She's got her Catherine wheels on

Go kindly with him
To his blind apparition
Whose face creases up with age gone grey
You'll be back here one day

She was always the first to say gone
She's got her Catherine wheels on
Always the first to say gone
She's got her Catherine wheels on, wheels on

Catherine wheels
Catherine wheels
Catherine wheels

She's gone, vanished in the night
Broke off the logic of life
He woke, tore the covers back
Found he was empty inside
So they were told when the moon would rise
The best time to leave with your soul

She's gone up towards the light
Watching her whole life unfold
Bruises come up dark
So strong was his hold on her
Regarded by some as his slave
He spoke in a stranger's tongue
To spare us and drive you away
Bruises come up dark

TOGETHER ALONE

N. FINN / B. WEHI / M. HART

Together alone
Above and beneath
We were as close
As anyone can be
Now you are gone
Far away from me
As is once
Will always be
Together alone

Anei ra maua
E piri tahi nei
E noha tahi nei
Ko maua anake
Kei runga a Rangi
Ko papa kei raro
E mau tonu nei
Kia mau tonu ra

Together alone
Shallow and deep
Holding our breath
Paying death no heed
I'm still your friend
When you are in need
As is once
Will always be
Earth and sky
Moon and sea

[Maori Chant]

Anei ra maua
E piri tahi nei
E noha tahi nei
Ko maua anake
Kei runga a Rangi
Ko papa kei raro
E mau tonu nei
Kia mau tonu ra

[Translation]

Here we are together
In a very close embrace
Being together
Just us alone

Rangi the sky-father is above
The earth-mother is below
Our love for one another
Is everlasting

ODDZ AND ENZ

THINGS
N. FINN

You stand around, I'll scream and shout, for your
    pleasure
You hand me round, all your friends, makes them
    happy

And you ask me what it's all for
It's as simple as the ABC law
What the hell you asking me for
Cause everything I do I do for you

We'll entertain, every night, where's the party
As me to sing, pass the drinks, where's the money

And you ask me what it's all for
It's as simple as the ABC law
What the hell you asking me for
Cause everything I do I do for you, you, you
Everything I do I do for you, you, you

REAR ENZ

Late In Rome

N. FINN / R. MURDOCH

Tired eyes remember the spotlights
Tired eyes remember the late nights
With ladies on my arms, nights of passion
Is it too long ago when you could hear them say

Serge he's a dancer
Knows each dramatic pose
Rolls the ladies they fall over
His future's in his toes

Who of you would know me now
You lovers once cherished and gone
But I've slept late in Rome before
And my story many times has been sung

Serge he's a dancer
Knows each dramatic pose
Rolls the ladies they fall over
His future's in his toes

Where are you now flirting lover
You are with a young man it seems
And all those times we had together
A part in his playful scene

Serge he's a dancer
Knows each dramatic pose
Rolls the ladies they fall over
His future's in his toes

BEFORE AND AFTER

In Love With It All

N. FINN / T.FINN

God's white beard hung down
Sacrilegious town
Sleek nostalgia blonde
The one you had your eyes on
As you came back from the altar
Your head was all a-gaga

In love with it all
In love with it all
In love with it all
With it all

Brothers come to blows
White shirt all aglow
All laid out ahead
Just like the family photos
That fall out of the suitcase
And wear the same expression

In love with it all
In love with it all
In love with it all
With it all

To score the highest hilltop
To turn the angry river
Leave ripples on the surface

In love with it all
In love with it all
In love with it all
With it all

STRANGENESS AND CHARM

N. FINN / T. FINN

You and I we circle each other
The truth is a powerful magnet
And beauty draws you in to her dragnet
Then she sets you free

Strangeness and charm
That's what you are
Strangeness and charm
That's what you are

We can't separate 'cos we annihilate
Fortune and favour come too late
Break down the pieces until you're left
With nothing else

Strangeness and charm
That's what you are
Strangeness and charm
That's what you are

Particles of flying dust go by
A hundred billion million atoms
I don't think I want to know
What you are is no more than
Strangeness and charm
What you need is to share the air
That Einstein breathes
What you are is no more than
Strangeness and charm

I think I want to know you
I don't think I want to know
I don't think I want to know

Strangeness and charm
That's what you are
Come on and share it with me
Share it with me

WOODFACE

Chocolate Cake

N. FINN / T. FINN

Not everyone in New York would pay to see Andrew
   Lloyd Webber
May his trousers fall down as he bows to the queen and
   the crown
I don't know what tune the orchestra played
But it went by me sickly, sentimental

Can I have another piece of chocolate cake
Tammy Baker's got a lot on her plate
Can I buy another cheap Picasso fake
Andy Warhol must be laughing in his grave

The band of the night take you to ethereal heights over
   dinner
And you wander the streets never reaching the heights
   that you seek
And the sugar that dripped from the violin's bow made
   the children go crazy
Put a hole in the tooth of a hag

Can I have another piece of chocolate cake
Tammy Baker must be losing her faith, yeah
Can I buy another cheap Picasso fake
Andy Warhol must be laughing in his grave

And dogs are on the road, we're all tempting fate
Cars are shooting by with no number plates
And here comes Mrs Hairy Legs

I saw Elvis Presley walk out of a Seven Eleven
And a woman gave birth to a baby and then bowled 257

Now the excess of fat on your American bones
Will cushion the impact as you sink like a stone

Can I have another piece of chocolate cake
Tammy Baker, Tammy Baker
Can I buy another cheap Picasso fake
Cheap Picasso, cheap Picasso fake

Can I have another piece of chocolate cake
Kathy Straker boy could she lose some weight
Can I buy another slice of real estate
Liberace must be laughing in his grave

It's Only Natural

N. FINN

Ice will melt, water will boil
You and I can shake off this mortal coil
It's bigger than us
You don't have to worry about it

Ready or not, here comes the drop
You feel lucky when you know where you are
You know it's gonna come true
Here in your arms I remember

It's only natural that I should want to be there with you
It's only natural that you should feel the same way too

It's easy when you don't try going on first impressions
Man in a cage has made his confession now
You've seen me at my worst
And it won't be the last time I'm down there

I want you to know I feel completely at ease
Read me like a book that's fallen down
Between your knees, please
Let me have my way with you

It's only natural that I should want to be there with you
It's only natural that you should feel the same way too
It's circumstantial, it's nothing written in the sky
And we don't have to try

But we'll be shaking like mud, buildings of glass
Sink in to the bay, they'll be under the rocks again
You don't have to say
I know you're afraid

It's only natural that I should want to be there with you
It's only natural that you should feel the same way too
It's circumstantial, it's something I was born to
It's only natural, can I help it if I want to

Fall At Your Feet

N. FINN

I'm really close tonight
And I feel like I'm moving inside her
Lying in the dark
And I think that I'm beginning to know her
Let it go
I'll be there when you call

Whenever I fall at your feet
You let your tears rain down on me
Whenever I touch your slow turning pain

You're hiding from me now
There's something in the way that you're talking
Words don't sound right
But I hear them all moving inside you, go
I'll be waiting when you call

Whenever I fall at your feet
Won't you let your tears rain down on me
Whenever I touch your slow turning pain

The finger of blame has turned upon itself
And I'm more than willing to offer myself
Do you want my presence or need my help
Who knows where that might lead
I fall

Whenever I fall at your feet
Would you let your tears rain down on me
Whenever I fall, ever I fall

Tall Trees

N. FINN / T. FINN

Watch out big ships are waiting
Salt frozen on your cheek
I saw a girl and boy arriving
And a steamer put out to sea

Tall tree
Stand in the distance
Remember
When you were green
Don't wipe
The salt from your skin
You must keep running the distance

Sun sleeps on misty morning
Light years from channel three
I feel halfway to zero
Call me a hero I might just agree

Tall tree
Stand in the distance
Remember
When you were green
Don't wipe
The salt from your skin
You must keep running the distance

And the roses you grow
Have a powerful scent
They'll be breaking your heart
By the morning

I feel halfway to zero
Call me a hero I might just agree

Tall tree
Stand in the distance
Remember
When you were green
Don't wipe
The salt from your skin
Tall tree
Tall tree
Don't wipe
The salt from your skin
You must keep running the distance
Tall tree

WEATHER WITH YOU

N. FINN / T. FINN

Walking 'round the room singing stormy weather
At 57 Mount Pleasant Street
Well it's the same room but everything's different
You can fight the sleep but not the dream

Things ain't cooking in my kitchen
Strange affliction wash over me
Julius Caesar and the Roman Empire
Couldn't conquer the blue sky

Well there's a small boat made of china
It's going nowhere on the mantlepiece
Well do I lie like a loungeroom lizard
Or do I sing like a bird released

Everywhere you go
Always take the weather with you

WHISPERS AND MOANS

N. FINN

Dull, dull grey
The colour of our times
Cool, cool space
That I still hope to find
Far beyond the veil
The sound of whispers and moans

Slow, time bomb
The clamour of the street
I hear this town
It never goes to sleep
And I will catch the taxi driver
Weeping like a wounded beast

Then I wake up in your room
To share one piece of your life
When tomorrow comes we may not be here at all
Without your whispers and moans
Cause here you come to carry me home
Here you come to carry me home

Love that sound
Time erase
Tension wheels
Cool heels
Won't ya come on open the bid before too long

Then I wake up in your room
To share one piece of your life
I'd give anything to be a fly upon the wall

And hear your whispers and moans
I'd like to hear your whispers and moans
Here you come to carry me

We are the mirrors
Of each other in a lifetime of suspicion
Cleansed in a moment a flash of recognition
You gave your life for it
Worth its weight in gold
And growing empires and art collectors
And Alan's sound investments
Will one day be forgotten
One day be forgotten, yeah

Four Seasons In One Day

N. FINN / T. FINN

Four seasons in one day
Lying in the depths of your imagination
Worlds above and worlds below
The sun shines on the black clouds hanging over the
    domain

Even when you're feeling warm
The temperature could drop away
Like four seasons in one day

Smiling as the shit comes down
You can tell a man from what he has to say
Everything gets turned around
And I will risk my neck again, again

You can take me where you will
Up the creek and through the mill
All the things you can't explain
Four seasons in one day

Blood dries up
Like rain, like rain
Fills my cup
Like four seasons in one day

It doesn't pay to make predictions
Sleeping on an unmade bed
Finding out wherever there is comfort there is pain
Only one step away
Like four seasons in one day

Blood dries up
Like rain, like rain
Fills my cup
Like four seasons in one day

THERE GOES GOD

N. FINN / T. FINN

What'll I tell him
When he comes to me for absolution
Wouldn't you know it
Hope I don't make a bad decision

Cause I'd like to believe
That there is a god
Why sinful angels
Suffer for love
I'd like to believe
In the terrible truth
In the beautiful lie

Like to know you
But in this town I can't get arrested
If you know me
Why don't you tell me what I'm thinking

Hey don't look now
But there goes God
In his sexy pants
And his sausage dog
And he can't stand
Beelzebub
Cause he looks so good in black, in black

FAME IS

N. FINN

Fork lightning in your hall
Break the skin when you break the fall
I'll be the one to fix it up

Love children of the new age
Just a hippy with a weekly wage
There's no rebellion just a chance to be lazy

When fame is in your blood
You follow the science of love
Wave the magic wand
And hang on

Now the rest of us are living in a daze
Keep thinkin' 'bout the choice to be made
Here come the handmaidens of end time

Lost treasure from a primitive race
All the lives written on your face
Can't fill the canyons of your mind

When fame is in your blood
You follow the science of love
Wave the magic wand
And hang on

Now you've changed
And jumbled the pieces you've changed
You're better before you talked
To a roomful of strangers
Here come the handmaidens of end time

When fame is in your blood
You follow the science of love
Wave the magic wand
All of your stars will fall
And all of your spells will break
So look out for number one
Fame is in your blood

ALL I ASK?

N. FINN / T. FINN

All I ask
Is to live each moment
Free from the last
Take the road forgotten
Don't leave me here
Oh, please let me stray
Far from familiar things

All I ask
Is to live each moment
All I ask
Is to live each moment
Free from the last

Strange roads
Going nowhere
Going nowhere in particular

All I ask
Is to live each moment
All I ask
Is to live each moment
Free from the last
Free from the last
All I ask

As Sure As I Am

N. FINN

Make your decision now
Rely on no help from above
Living is luxury
I want everything you throw out
I'll do anything you want to

Please let me go with you
I'll wear the smile on your face
Big, black and beautiful
I want it, everything you throw out
There must be something you can do without

Cause I am as sure as I am
I couldn't care less
For what might go wrong
And I'm as happy as sin
In a fear shaken world

I pity the rhino
Down there it's becoming extinct
Killed for a love potion
Sad thing looking like a dead flower
I want it, everything that you throw out

Cos I am as sure as I am
I couldn't care less
For what might go wrong
And I'm as happy as sin
In a fear shaken world

Don't wanna be there
Don't wanna be spared
I'll wear the smile on your face
I am as sure as I am

I couldn't care less
For what might go wrong
And I'm as happy as sin
In a fear shaken world, world,
Couldn't care less

She Goes On

N. FINN

Pretty soon you'll be able to remember her
Lying in the garden singing
Right where she'll always be
The door is always open

This is the place that I loved her
And these are the friends that she had
Long may the mountain ring
To the sound of her laughter
And she goes on and on

In her soft wind I will whisper
In her warm sun I will glisten
Till we see her once again
In a world without end

We owe it all to Frank Sinatra
The song was playing as she walked into the room
After the long weekend
They were a lifetime together

Appearing in the eyes of children
In the clear blue mountain view
They're colouring in the sky
And painting ladders to heaven
And she goes on

In her soft wind I will whisper
In her warm sun I will glisten
Till we see her once again
In a world without end

In her soft wind I will whisper
In her warm sun I will glisten
And I always will remember
In a world without end
She goes on
She goes on
She goes on

How Will You Go

N. FINN / T. FINN

Escape is on your mind again
Escape to a far away land
At times it seems there is no end
To long hard nights of drinking

How will you go, how will you go
Drive through the wind and the rain
Cover it up, cover it up
I'll find you a shelter to sleep in

I fell over on the couch again
But you know not all sleep is wasted
Your dreams are alcohol inspired
I can't find a better way to face it

How will you go, how will you go
Drive through the wind and the rain
Cover it up, cover it up
I'll find you a shelter to sleep in

And you know, I'll be fine
Just don't ask me how it's going
Gimme time, gimme time
Cause I want you to see
'Round the world, 'round the world
Is a tangled up necklace of pearls

How will you go, how will you go
Drive through the wind and the rain
Cover it up, cover it up
I'll find you a shelter to sleep in

TEMPLE OF LOW MEN

I Feel Possessed

N. FINN

She said I could never do that
But I know you can, you are in my dream
We are one person not two of a kind
And what was mine is now in your possession
I could feel you underneath my skin
As the wind rushed in
Sent the kitchen table crashing
She said nobody move
Or I'll bring the house down

I hardly know which way is up
Or which way down
People are strange God only knows
I feel possessed when you come around

It was one of those times
Wished I had a camera on me
Six foot off the ground
Well I know how that sounds
Look above you and beyond me too
That kind of view don't need an explanation
I'm not lying, not asking for anything
I just want to be there when it happens again

I hardly know which way is up
Or which way down
People are strange God only knows
I feel possessed when you come round

Whenever you invade my home
Everything I know flies out the window
It's above you and beyond me too
I don't want an explanation
But I'll be there when you bring the house down

I hardly know which way is up
Or which way down
People are strange God only knows
I feel possessed when you come round
People are strange
I feel possessed when you come round

KILL EYE

N. FINN

Kill eye tumbling come out of the sky
Kill eye a fiery retreat from the stars
Kill eye he came clambering over the wall
Kill eye halfway to hell and beyond

I wanna be forgiven
I wanna laugh with children
Won't you ever forgive me
Please please forgive me
I wanna hug my mother
And the sky above her
I want the earth to open up
And hold me

Kill eye shoot your way out of the bank
Kill eye watch the security guard
Kill eye separate a man from his life

I wanna be forgiven
I wanna laugh with children
I wanna ride the pony
Be your one and only friend
I will love you till the end

Kill eye half way to hell and beyond
I wanna hug my mother
And the sky above her
I want the earth to open up
I want the earth to open up

INTO TEMPTATION

N. FINN

You opened up your door
I couldn't believe my luck
You in your new blue dress
Taking away my breath
The cradle is soft and warm
Couldn't do me no harm
You're showing me how to give

Into temptation
Knowing full well the earth will rebel
Into temptation

In a muddle of nervous words
Could never amount to betrayal
The sentence is all my own
The price is to watch it fail
As I turn to go
You looked at me for half a second
An open invitation for me to go

Into temptation
Knowing full well the earth will rebel
Into temptation
Safe in the wide open arms of hell

We can go sailing in
Climb down
Lose yourself when you linger long
Into temptation
Right where you belong

The guilty get no sleep
In the last slow hours of morning
Experience is cheap
I should've listened to the warning
But the cradle is soft and warm

Into temptation
Knowing full well the earth will rebel
Into your wide open arms
No way to break the spell
Don't tell

Mansion In The Slums
N. FINN

I'd much rather have a caravan in the hills
Than a mansion in the slums
The taste of success only lasts you
Half an hour or less
But it loves you when it comes
And you laugh at yourself
While you're bleeding to death

I'd much rather have a trampoline in my front room
Than an isolation tank
I wish I was a million miles away
From the manager's door
There is trouble at the bank
You laugh at yourself
As you go deep into debt
Laugh at yourself
While he's breathing down your neck

Who can stop me
With money in my pocket
Sometimes I get it free
The best of both worlds
I'd much rather have a caravan in the hills
I'd much rather have a mansion ... in the hills
Than a mansion in the slums
Yeah I'd much rather ...
What I mean is, would you mind if I had it all
I'll take it when it comes
And you laugh at yourself

While you're bleeding to death
And somebody else is always
Breathing down your neck
Laugh at yourself
While he's hanging over your head
The best of both worlds
It'll soon be over

When You Come

N. FINN

When you come across the sea
Me like a beacon guiding you to safety
The sooner the better now
And when you come the hills
Will breathe like a baby
Pulled up heaving from the bottom of the ocean
The sooner the better now
When you come to cover me with your kisses
Fresh like a daisy chained up in a lion's den
I'll know you by the thunderclap
Pouring like a rain of blood to my emotions

And that is why
I stumble to my knees
And why underneath the heavens
With the stars burning and exploding
I know I could never let you down

When you come like an iceberg floating in darkness
Smashing my hull send me to the bottom of the sea
I should know you better now
When you come your majesty to entrap me
Prince of light receding
The sooner the better now
And when you come to cover me
With your kisses hard like armour
The sooner the better now
I'll know you by the thunderclap
Pouring like a rain of blood to my emotions

And that is why
I stumble to my knees
And why underneath the heavens
With the stars burning and exploding
I know I could never let you down

She came out of the water
Into my horizon
Like a cumulo nimbus
Coming in from a distance
Burning and exploding
Burning and exploding
Like a slow volcano
When you come
Cover the ground with ashes
When you come

Never Be The Same

N. FINN

Don't stand around
Like friends at a funeral
Eyes to the ground
It could've been you

Why do you weep
For the passing of ages
You slip with the back of your hand
You're taking it out on the one you love
I couldn't believe it

But we might still survive
And rise up through the maze
If you could change your life
And never be the same

How long must I wait
For you to release me
I pay for each mistake
While you suffer in silence
I could still have an easy life
But the lie ain't worth the living
Once more will I hear you say

We might still survive
And rise up through the maze
If you could change your life
And never be the same

Don't stand around
Like friends at a funeral
Eyes to the ground
Don't suffer in silence

Cause we might still survive
And rise up through the maze
If you could change your life
And never be the same
Every time I hear you
Never be the same
And every time I mess up
Never be the same

LOVE THIS LIFE

N. FINN

Seal my fate
I get your tongue in the mail
No one is wise
Until they see how it lies
Love this life
Don't wait till the next one comes
Pedal my faith
The wheels are still turning round, turn round

And maybe the day will come
When you'll never have to feel no pain
After all my complaining
Gonna love this life
Gonna love this life

And so they threw you in jail
Whatever you've done
It was a million to one
And don't you just love this life
When it's holding you down
Pedal my faith
The wheels are still turning round, turn round

So maybe the day will come
When you'll never have to feel no pain
After all my complaining
Gonna love this life
Gonna love this life

There's something that you can do
Even if you think that I hate you
Stop your complaining, leave me defenceless
When you love this life
Gotta love this life
Love this life though you'll never know why
Gonna love this life

Sister Madly

N. FINN

Now you're heading down to get someone
Should've done what he had to do years ago
The position is coming through
All the people that you're standing on
All the people that you're standing on
Now you're heading down to be someone
Someone that you've seen in a magazine
Your premonition is coming true
Oh baby you're not so green
No baby you're not so green
No baby you're nutso

Sister madly waking up the dead
You're systematically stepping on my head

Now you're heading down to find something
Something that you buried in your backyard
The position is coming through
From all the dirt that you're digging up
From all the dirt that you're digging up
Now you're heading down to be somewhere
Somewhere you imagined in your wildest dream
The opposition is coming through
From all the people that you're standing on
From all the people that you're standing on
Now you'd better take a firm hand

Sister madly waking up the dead
You're systematically stepping on my head

Now you're heading down to get someone
Someone that you should've had years ago
The position is coming through
All the people that you're standing on
All the people that you're standing on
You're hard to get a hand on

Sister madly waking up the dead
Systematically stepping on my head

In The Lowlands

N. FINN

Oh hell trouble is coming
Out here in panic and alarm
Black shapes gather in the distance
Looks like it won't take long

The first drops land on the window
The first sign that there's something wrong
Light rain and a head full of thunder
Which way, which way

Two days till I get to you
I'll be late if I ever get through
Where I go there'll be no kind welcome
Coming down upon me

Time will keep me warm
Feel my face
Now the insects swarm
In the lowlands
Fear will take the place of desire
And we will fan the flames on high
Try for heaven's sake

The sky fell underneath a blanket
The sun sank as the miles went by
Sit back with your head on the pillow
When you remember it makes you cry

Ghost cars on the freeway
Like friends that you thought you had
One by one they are disappearing

Time will keep me warm
Feel my face
Now the insects swarm
In the lowlands
Fear will take the place of desire
And we will fan the flames on high

BETTER BE HOME SOON

N. FINN

Somewhere deep inside
Something's got a hold on you
And it's pushing me aside
See it stretch on forever

I know I'm right
For the first time in my life
That's why I tell you
You'd better be home soon

Stripping back the coats
Of lies and deception
Back to nothingness
Like a week in the desert

I know I'm right
For the first time in my life
That's why I tell you
You'd better be home soon

So don't say no, don't say nothing's wrong
Cause when you get back home maybe I'll be gone

It would cause me pain
If we were to end it
But I could start again
You can depend on it

I know I'm right
For the first time in my life
That's why I tell you

You'd better be home soon
That's why I tell you
You'd better be home soon

BODY AND SOUL

You I Know

N. FINN

Some men have muscle
They are muscle bound
And on display
Some men have money
And a few of them
Think they can own me

But it's you I know
And no one else will do
Yes it's you I know
With all you put me through
When I was drifting down
You pulled me up again
And it's you I know
You'll love me to the end

Some men think they're funny
But when the laughing stops
You're on your own
Some are familiar
Before their real intentions
Are fully shown
Sometimes I wonder
If I know myself
As well as I know you

But it's you I know
And no one else will do
Yes it's you I know
With all you put me through

When I was drifting down
You pulled me up again
And it's you I know
You love me to the end

You could be anything
You could be anything you want
You could be everywhere
You could be everywhere at once
You could have anyone
You don't need me to get you going
You could have anyone

Your sea is full to overflowing
I've seen them walking
Through a market place in Florence
I've heard them singing
In a foreign place in Spanish
Sometimes I wonder
If I know myself
As well as I know you

But it's you I know
And no one else will do
Yes it's you I know
With all you put me through
When I was drifting down
You pull me up again
And it's you I know
You love me to the end

CROWDED HOUSE

MEAN TO ME

N. FINN

She came all the way from America
Had a blind date with destiny
And the sound of Te Awamutu
Had a truly sacred ring
Now her parents are divorced
And her friend's committing suicide

I could not escape
A plea from the heart
You know what it means to me
She said don't walk away
I'm down on my knees
So please don't be mean to me

So I talked to you for an hour
In the bar of a small town hotel
You asked me what I was thinking
I was thinking of a padded cell
With a black and white T.V.
To stop us from getting lonely

I could not escape
A plea from the heart
You know what it means to me
She said don't walk away
I'm down on my knees
So please don't be mean to me
No, I could not escape
A plea from the heart
Mysterious sympathy

I couldn't wait for a chance
To walk out the door
You know what it means to me

I saw you lying in the arms of a poet
I heard him tell you t … tantalising lies
Well whad'd'ya know, whad'd'ya know

I could not escape
You're down on the floor
You know what it means to me
I couldn't wait for a chance
To walk out the door
Mean …
You know what it means
In the arms of a poet
You know what it means

WORLD WHERE YOU LIVE
N. FINN

Here's someone now who's got the muscle
His steady hand could move a mountain
Expert in bed but come on now
There must be something missing
That golden one leads a double life
You'll find out
But I don't know where you go
Do you climb into space
To the world where you live
The world where you live

So here we lie against each other
These four walls can never hold us
We're looking for wide open spaces
High above the kitchen
And we're strangers here
On our way to some other place
But I don't know where you go
Do you climb into space
To the world where you live
The world where you live
The world where you live

When friends come round
You might remember and be sad
Behind their eyes is unfamiliar
Do you climb into space
To the world where you live
The world where you live ...

NOW WE'RE GETTING SOMEWHERE

N. FINN

It never used to be that bad
But neither was it great
Somewhere in the middle then
Content and much too safe
Ooh tell me please
Why it takes so long
To realise when there's something wrong

Lay me out with your heart
Now we're gettin' somewhere
Push me back to the start
Now we're gettin' somewhere
Take me out, let me breathe
Now we're gettin' somewhere
When I'm with you I don't care
Where it is I'm falling

There's money in the Bible Belt
Hugs for daddy too
Three wishes for eternity
We've got some work to do
Ooh tell me please, tell me what went wrong
Cause I believe there is something wrong

Lay me out with your heart
Now we're gettin' somewhere
Push me back to the start
Now we're gettin' somewhere
Take me out let me breathe
Now we're gettin' somewhere

When I'm with you I don't care
Where it is I'm falling

When you took me to your room
I swear I said surrender
When you opened up your mouth
I saw the words fall out
Though nothing much has changed
I swear I will surrender
There is pain in my heart
We can choose what we choose to believe

DON'T DREAM IT'S OVER

N. FINN

There is freedom within, there is freedom without
Try to catch the deluge in a paper cup
There's a battle ahead, many battles are lost
But you'll never see the end of the road
While you're travelling with me

Hey now, hey now
Don't dream it's over
Hey now, hey now
When the world comes in
They come, they come
To build a wall between us
We know they won't win

Now I'm towing my car, there's a hole in the roof
My possessions are causing me suspicion but there's no
    proof
In the paper today tales of war and of waste
But you turn right over to the T.V. page

Hey now, hey now
Don't dream it's over
Hey now, hey now
When the world comes in
They come, they come
To build a wall between us
We know they won't win

Now I'm walking again to the beat of a drum
And I'm counting the steps to the door of your heart

Only shadows ahead barely clearing the roof
Get to know the feeling of liberation and relief

Hey now, hey now
Don't dream it's over
Hey now, hey now
When the world comes in
They come, they come
To build a wall between us
Don't ever let them win

LOVE YOU TILL THE DAY I DIE

N. FINN

There's closets in my head where dirty things are kept
That never see the light of day
I want to drag them out, go for a walk
Just to see the look that's on your face
Sometimes I can't be straight, I don't want to hurt you
So forgive me if I tell a lie
Sometimes I come on cold but don't believe it
I will love you till the day I die

I believe in doing things backwards
Take heed, start doing things in reverse

Here comes trouble, there's nothing wrong when
    I relax
I'm talking to myself you're coming with me
Teaching you how to distort the facts
Sometimes I can't be straight I don't want to hurt you
So forgive me if I tell a lie
Sometimes I come on cold but don't believe it
I will love you till the day I die

I believe in doing things backwards
Take heed, start doing things in reverse

Frost on the window pane, the sound of pouring rain
All makes me glad of you
Though I am far away I am always with you

Know the answer before you know the question
Pull yourself together, baby, push with all your might

I'm all alone, always alone
Though I am far away
I am always with you

SOMETHING SO STRONG

N. FINN / M. FROOM

Love can make you weep
Can make you run for cover
Roots that spread so deep
Bring life to frozen ground

Something so strong
Could carry us away
Something so strong
Could carry us today

Turning in my sleep
Love can leave you cold
The taste of jealousy
Is like a lust for gold

Something so strong
Could carry us away
Something so strong
Could carry us today

I've been feeling so much older
Frame me and hang me on the wall
I've seen you fall into the same trap
This thing is happening to us all

Something so strong
Could carry us away
Something so strong
Could carry us today

HOLE IN THE RIVER

N. FINN / E. RAYNER

There's a hole in the river where my auntie lies
From the land of the living to the air and sky
Left her car by the river left her shoes beside
Through the thorns and the bushes I hope she was ...

Dreaming of glory
Miles above the mountains and plains
Free at last

We were touched by a cold wind, my father and I
The sound of desperate breathing her fear inside us all
She was coming to see him but something changed her
    mind
Drove her down to the river
There is no return

There's a hole in the river where a memory lies
From the land of the living to the air and sky
She was coming to see him
But something changed her mind
Drove her down to the river
There is no return

Can't Carry On

N. FINN

Why do I kid myself
Why do I scream for pleasure
It's four in the morning should know better
But she can weave a spell
Want it to last forever
Making me feel like somebody special

Can't carry on this way (just go to sleep)
Before it gets too late (just go to sleep)
Doing damage to my brain
Well here we go again

Though I look everywhere
I never seem to find it
Always a shadow around a corner
Drown it in alcohol
Stuck in the elevator
Hard to remember in the morning

Can't carry on this way (just go to sleep)
Before it gets too late (just go to sleep)
Doing damage to my brain
Well here we go again

Tell you about myself
If you're in the mood to listen
Baby you don't know who you're kissing
This is a lonely world
You are a strange companion
When you get what you wanted
You want to leave

Honestly I want to free myself
From the burden of inaction
Honestly I want to raise myself
To any plane I can imagine

Can't carry on this way (just go to sleep)
Before it gets too late (just go to sleep)
Doing damage to my brain
Well here we go again

Tombstone

N. FINN

Look at all the plans I made
Falling down like scraps of paper
I will leave them where they lie to remind me
From the past a rumour comes
Don't let it keep draggin' you down
Throw the memory in an open fire
You'll be free

Roll back the tombstone
Let the saints appear
Roll back the tombstone
Make a new man out of me

Beware the passenger
The train already left the station
We are neither at home nor at work
We are moving
Listen to the howling of steel
A face betraying no emotion
Like you never had a chance to be
Wild and free

Roll back the tombstone
Let the saints appear
Roll back the tombstone
Till the Lone Ranger rides again
Rides again in your mind

Rode across the open plain
All the way and back again

THAT'S WHAT I CALL LOVE

N. FINN / P. HESTER

You take away my air
You make my lungs collapse
I die tonight

Feeling devastated
That's what I call
Livin' in your memory
That's what I call
Tired and deflated
That's what I call love

I tidy up your room
You tidy up my life
Show me the door

I'm abandoned here
I'm warm to the core
I can feel
You sink I swim
We never got in that deep
You bend I break
I die tonight

Feeling devastated
That's what I call
Hangin' on and fallin' over
That's what I call
Tired and deflated
That's what I call love

I got a little room
The air's still pretty bad
I die tonight

Feeling devastated
That's what I call
Hangin' on and fallin' over
That's what I call
Tired and deflated
That's what I call
Feeling devastated
That's
Livin' with a vacuum cleaner
What
Sweepin' up your memory
I call love

SEE YA ROUND

I Walk Away

N. FINN

You came
Out of this world to me
My life
Parted like the Red Sea
We flowed
Easy between the rocks and stones
Never seemed to stop us
The years
Ended in confusion
Don't ask me I don't know what happened
But I am
A man with a mission
Must be the devil I don't know

It's hard to let go
Of all that we know
As I walk away from you
Hurled from my home
Into the unknown
As I walk away from you

Reveal whatever you desire
To you it may be death defying
Black day
In the coldness of winter
Black words
Slipping off my tongue
I say forget it—it's over
As a dark cloud covered up the sun

It's hard to let go
Of all that we know
As I walk away from you
The sun always sets
No room for regrets
As I walk away from you

Give it to me
Give it to me
Your inspiration
Give to receive
Find all we need
As I walk away

Breakin' My Back

N. FINN

Come my girl, you could cure almost anything
Take this man, use your power give him energy
Pick me up, stop me feeling sorry for myself
There are times, when almost everybody needs some
   help

Cause I've been breakin' my back
With the weight of it all
And I've been breakin' my back

If I am strong, why do I falter?
Scratch my back and tickle my toes
Sing the song that we all know
Watch my mind become a desert where nothing
   grows

And I've been breakin' my back
With the weight of it all
Yes, I've been breakin' my back
But I ain't giving it up
I ain't letting it go
But it's been breakin' my back

Stay with me
A fool aspires
To raise himself
Out of the mire

I've been breakin' my back
And I been breakin' up too

Yes I'm a pain in the neck
But I can only improve

And I been breaking my back ...

KIA KAHA ('FOREVER STRONG')

N. FINN

(Kia kaha)
I left you in the shelter
On a wet Waikato day
The rain came like a flood
Washed our stamping ground away
And so the ties were broken
Our situation's changed
I wonder to myself now
If we are still the same

We used to laugh at the words of the old school song
But now I hope that you will be ever strong (kia kaha)

We gathered in the basement
Like some religious sect
A band of idle dreamers
In a small town safety net
It's been as long as five years
Since we were face to face
We're feeling for the first time
Should have something to show for our age

We used to laugh at the words of the old school song
But now I hope that you will be ever strong (Kia kaha)
When I left town I thought an angel watched over me
It was a shock to find the devil inside me, beside me
    (Kia kaha)

(Kia kaha)
Where did it go, I never noticed it passing

(Kia kaha)
Already it's a long time ago …

ONE MOUTH IS FED

N. FINN

There must be a lot of pain
For the happiness I feel today
The balance can be cruel sometimes
Can turn you 'round the other way
I lifted up my head from sleep
Linger in the scent of a dream
Someone must be crying now
To make me laugh in sympathy

Well I could be wrong, you could be right
As one mouth is fed, another is denied
Why all the tears, we're crying with delight

As we lay in between the sheets
Ships are sinking in the bay
Find yourself a love to keep
And someone else will have to pay
I lifted up my head from sleep
Linger in the scent of a dream
Someone must be crying now
To make me laugh in sympathy

Well I could be wrong, you could be right
As one mouth is fed, another is denied
Why all the tears, we're crying with delight

I could be wrong
I could be right, I could be wrong

Well I could be wrong, you could be right
As one mouth is fed, another is denied
Why all the tears, we're crying with delight
As one mouth is fed, another is denied
I could be wrong, you could be right
I could be right, you could be wrong

Voices

N. FINN

Wander through the library
Volumes of the deceased
There's no happy endings
History has been cruel
Feel the blood of ages
Flowing through my veins
Still there is no reason
I wonder what's coming

I hear voices
Leading me on
The wise and the strong

Wander through the forest
Losing track of time
Lessons in green and gold
Been growing on for years

I hear voices
Leading me on
Urging me on

I hear voices
Leading me on
Urging me on
The wise and the strong

Years Go By

N. FINN / E. RAYNER

She gets up in the afternoon
The sun will set behind her
When the twilight comes
The magic one, will gaze on you

Seconds last for hours all evening
This purple room is breathing
To the milky way I turn my gaze
It's a mystery

Years go by, wonder what you did
Yet in a minute you can change your life
All depends on your state of mind
One thing to be sure of is we live and die

Fear and doubt no longer harbour lies
Love not grow old where we reside
'Tis enough for now to set you down
And gaze on you

Years go by, wonder what you did
Yet in a minute you can change your life
All depends on your state of mind
One thing to be sure of is we live and die
(repeat chorus to fade)

CONFLICTING EMOTIONS

BULLET BRAIN AND CACTUS HEAD

N. FINN

Send a message to the brain
Two men climbing down opposite poles
The one with hair upon his face
Sprouting like the weeds on his soul
The other is a law unto himself
His brain is like a lump of steel
And they'd love to break each other up
Into tiny pieces

It's strange how they're always together
Bullet Brain and Cactus Head
Always beating heads together
Bullet Brain and Cactus Head

Watch them fall into the dirt
Desperate to make a point
No trace of human doubt
Confrontation they can never avoid
Despising what they've both become
Always looking for someone to blame
They think they're worlds apart
But they're exactly the same
Always will be

It's strange how they're always together
Bullet Brain and Cactus Head
Always beating heads together
Bullet Brain and Cactus Head
Which one of you's the liar
Bullet Brain and Cactus Head

Fanatic believers, obsessive achievers
Yippees and yahoos, felons and fiends
Preachers and leeches, offenders, defenders
All on their way down to the depth of extremes
Pip-squeaking passion to head-on collision
Too set in your ways to give way or concede
Oh my, oh my, oh my, what will become of the macho
    pretender and his enemy

And it's strange how they're always together
Bullet Brain and Cactus Head
Always beating heads together
Bullet Brain and Cactus Head
Which one of you's the liar
Bullet Brain and Cactus Head
Rise up from the mire or wake up in a sea of red ...

THE DEVIL YOU KNOW

N. FINN

I long to see the other side of things
Hung on the cliff, in search of something big
I can't look down, I can only retreat
Who knows one day I'll dive into the sea

Here we all are sitting like fools
Stuck by the rules of fate
Is what we are what we've grown to believe
Better the devil you know

Live for the day we throw caution to the wind
All we need is the courage to begin
I might get hurt but never be scared again
At once to feel the pleasure and the pain

Into the city, into the city every day
Into the city, piling through the factory gates
It's not easy, it's not easy to escape
All the decisions that you've already made

I long to see the other side of things
Hung on the cliff, in search of something big
I can't look down, I can only retreat
Who knows one day I'll dive into the sea

Here we all are sitting like fools
Stuck by the rules of fate
Is what we are what we've grown to believe
Better the devil you know

MESSAGE TO MY GIRL

N. FINN

I don't want to say I love you
That would give away too much
(It's) hip to be detached and precious
The only thing you feel is vicious

I don't wanna say I want you
Even though I want you so much
It's wrapped up in conversation
It's whispered in a hush
Though I'm frightened by the word
Think it's time that it was heard

No more empty self-possession
Vision swept under the mat
It's no new year's resolution
It's more than that

And now I wake up happy
Warm in a lover's embrace
No one else can touch us
While we're in this place
So I'll sing it to the world
This simple message to my girl

No more empty self-possession
Vision swept under the mat
It's no new year's resolution
It's more than that

Though I'm frightened by the word
Think it's time I made it heard
So I sing it to the world
Simple message to my girl

No more empty self-possession
Vision swept under the mat
It's no new year's resolution
It's more than that

No there's nothing quite as real
As a touch of your sweet hand
I can't spend the rest of my life
Buried in the sand

No Mischief

N. FINN

No mischief, no mischief, no mischief
I don't need the aggravation
This ain't no time for foolin'
Let's get down to business
No mischief, no mischief, no mischief
I don't need the aggravation
No foolin', let's get down to business

There's a crowd outside
That's screaming for your blood
They want action now
From a man whose name is mud

They don't want no mischief, no mischief, no mischief
I don't need the aggravation
This ain't no time for foolin'
No horseplay, it's passé
Let's get down to business (all right)
No mischief, no mischief, no mischief
You're a constant irritation
The power goes to your head
So go get your brain read
Or you'll be out of business

Private profiteer
Our loss is your gain
The things that we revere
You're pouring down the drain
It's no game
When you are a leader

People want to swear by you
So swear by the truth

Still I live in hope
That you might disappear
Off the face of the globe
We won't miss you round here
Have no fear

No mischief, no mischief, no mischief
This ain't no time for foolin'
No horseplay, it's passé
Let's get down to business (No mischief, no mischief)
No mischief, no mischief, no mischief
I don't need the aggravation
The power goes to your head
So go get your brain read
Or you'll be out of business
No mischief, no I don't want no mischief

OUR DAY

N. FINN

Let our love create another life
It's growing even as we speak
He don't know what's waiting for him here
Suspended in his dream sleep
His mother's all around him
His father's just a sound to him, singing gently
We have promised him a future
So I'm hoping that tomorrow
Is, was, and will ever be

And we're waiting now
Waiting for our child to come
The old age is near the end
The new one's just begun

There's a face that I will come to love
That I have never seen before
There's a brain that's absolutely free
From any kind of conscious thought
You are me, and you are she
It won't be long 'til we meet
And we'll be going on a journey
In a flimsy paper boat upon a stormy sea

And so we're waiting now
Waiting for our child to come
The old age is near the end
The new one's just begun

Yes we're waiting now
For something burning far away
Tear the old age down for good
Welcome the young one

I'm shaking like a leaf
Wound up like a spring tonight
You say this ain't no place for children
Oh God, I hope that what we've done is right
Am I vain to feel as if the world
Owes anything at all to me
Searching, burning, tossing and turning
Desperately

And so we're waiting now
Waiting for our child to come
Can't imagine what the future holds
Just hoping there is one

Yes we're waiting now
For something burning far away
Tear the old age down for good
Welcome the young one

Hear this my son, I promise you the best that we can
do
We love, we love, we love, we love, we love, we love
you ...

STRAIT OLD LINE

N. FINN

This could be heaven, or this could be hell
Life could be falling down a bottomless well
I stumble to the left, I stumble to the right
I fumble for the switch of a disconnected light
(Stay with it) don't let temptation be your load
(Stay with it) there are bandits on the road

Don't look to the left
Don't look to the right
Just follow that strait old line
Don't look to the left
Don't look to the right
Just follow that strait old line

The road of ambition, is a casualty trail
Press gangs wait to ambush
The weak and weary (stay with it)
But I had to explore the light and dark
to see the sharp and flat
There's a hundred or more good reasons
not to ever turn your back

Don't look to the left
Don't look to the right
Just follow that strait old line
Don't look to the left
Don't look to the right
Just follow that strait old line

TIME AND TIDE

Take A Walk

N. FINN

Time to slip out of my back door
Sunrise dancing on my wall
Heading down off beaten tracks
Trying to get that feeling back

I could take a walk again
Up a mountain to a stream
Standing on the open rock
Looking out over the sea
Funny when we move ahead
Never worry what we leave behind
I could always find some peace
In the back of beyond

Kind voice from yesterday
Give love fill up every space
But now I laugh at simple truth
Sneer and frown like we all do

When the long night awakes
With memories a midnight feast
Feel the boy in me escape
There's a field of frost beneath my feet
Run, never tire, run boy, forever and ever

I could take a walk again
Up a mountain to a stream
Standing on the open rock
Looking out over the sea
Funny when we moved ahead

Never worry what we leave behind
Remember what a friend of mine said
You gotta be kind

Giant Heartbeat

N. FINN

Heartbeat
Bearing down
On our world
It never sleeps

Feel like a Zephyr harmonising with a flute
Notes are rising in familiar twos and threes
The time of yearning is the same at any age
The back is bending and the sky is growing pale

Sun up sun down fade to a lookalike
Hearts and souls move together in time

One step forward is a leap for all mankind
Old man river smiles on all he leaves behind
Ooh when temptation brings you down
I say you better spread yourself around
Red limbs, my body's torn apart
The boy's hand will squeeze the giant's heart

Sun up sun down fade to a lookalike
Hearts and souls move together in time
If anybody's listening, a giant heartbeat is fading

Fire burns
Water drowns
Hate kills
Our homes
Faith helps
Love heals

Sun up sun down fade to a lookalike
Hearts and souls move together in time
If anybody's listening
If anybody's listening
Is anybody listening, a giant heartbeat is fading

Hello Sandy Allen

N. FINN

Hello Sandy Allen
The world's tallest woman
We made friends in New York
Don't know if you'll remember
I'm bound to say I felt uneasy
When I first laid eyes on you
But I liked the way you talked
Like a live in hoper
Towering over our heads
In more ways than one
The hand that shook my hand was awesome
It still amazes me

Hope you're happy Sandy Allen
Hope your garden is blooming
We're all staring at the mirror
Tryin' to put our faces on
Appearance never held you back
Must be when you're number one
You don't have to try so hard

Hello Sandy Allen, hello Sandy Allen, hello ...

Hope you're happy Sandy Allen
Hope your garden is blooming
We're all staring at the mirror
Tryin' to put our faces on
Appearance never held you back
Must be when you're number one
You don't have to try so hard

Log Cabin Fever

N. FINN

Downstairs in the cellar drums are beating
Wounded, no discomfort, emotions bleeding
In the river alone, always alone, out of my depth
Headlong to the ocean will I sink or swim

Heard them tell the story of mad old Jim
Found him in his cabin with his head caved in
Waiting out the winter was a little too much for him

It's cold out, hear the wind howl down the chimney
Wish I could just cry out to someone, help
But we live in isolation of the cruellest kind
Scared to show our colours to the world

Time to break away from my condition
Rejoin the human race, see what I'm missing
Try to face the day my private passion
Is eating me away

Log cabin fever
It's a remote possibility
Log cabin fever
It's an impossible delivery
Log cabin fever
It's not an impossibility

Frenzy (A&M Version)

HOLY SMOKE
N. FINN

Holy smoke good God almighty
Vandals, murderers and thieves
I just woke up with the strangest feeling
There's someone here with me

Feel my heart
The fear of God written in my face
In the dark
Over there by the fireplace
The shadows fall much too close for comfort

Here all night the sun deserts you
Dark skies overhead
Candles lit and measures taken
Brave new worlds we tread

It's all I can do to keep from running away
Get me out of this place
Too young to lose
I've been sleeping with one eye open too long

Carried Away

N. FINN

Breathless home with excitement
I'll kick my shoes off
Get into the groove
Dancing I drift with my eyes closed
Hearing that voice again
Singing that strange melody

I get slowly carried away
Slowly carried away

All day I can hear her calling
That woman I've never met
Keeps leading me on

I get slowly carried away
Slowly carried away
I get slowly carried away
Slowly carried away
I get slowly carried away
Slowly carried away

I'm told that it's evergreen
I've listened but never seen
I've laid awake all night
Just putting the whole world right
It's terrible but true

I get carried away with you

CORROBOREE

History Never Repeats

N. FINN

History never repeats
I tell myself before I go to sleep
Don't say the words you might regret
I've lost before, you know I can't forget

There was a girl I used to know
She dealt my love a savage blow
I was so young, too blind to see
But anyway that's history

(I say) history never repeats
I tell myself before I go to sleep
Don't say the words you might regret
I've lost before, you know I can't forget

You say I always play the fool
I can't go on if that's the rule
Better to jump than hesitate
I need a change and I can't wait

History never repeats
I tell myself before I go to sleep
And there's a light shining in the dark
Leading me on towards a change of heart

History never repeats
I tell myself before I go to sleep

And there's a light shining in the dark
Leading me on towards a change of heart

Deep in the night it's all so clear
I lie awake with great ideas
Lurking about in no-man's land
I think at last I understand

History never repeats
I tell myself before I go to sleep
And there's a light shining in the dark
Leading me on towards a change of heart

IRIS

N. FINN

She's unaware, she'll never see me stare
Standing in the safety of my room
Oh I don't know, whether she comes or goes
But I know I'll be seeing her quite soon

Ooh Iris
The girl with the lovely name
I feel desirous
I got that girl to blame
Ooh Iris

I'll be brave, put all my fears away
I'm hoping that I get the chance to meet her
Sun or rain, I wait here every day
I wonder if I'll get the chance to kiss her

Ooh Iris
I'm stuck at the window pane
I feel desirous
I got that girl to blame
Ooh Iris

Ooh Iris
The girl with the lovely name
I feel desirous
I got that girl to blame
Ooh Iris

ONE STEP AHEAD

N. FINN

One step ahead of you
Stay in motion, keep an open mind
Love is a race won by two
Your emotion, my solitude
If I stop I could lose my head
So I'm losing you instead
Either way I'm confused
You slow me down, what can I do?
There's one particular way I have to choose

One step ahead of you
Always someone, makes it hard to move
She says, boy I want you to stay
But I save it all for another day
If I stop I could lose my head
But I'm ready for romance
Either way I'm confused
I don't know what I'm s'posed to do
I can only stay
One step ahead of you

Stop, I confess sometimes
I don't know where I'm going
Part of me stays with you,
I'm slowing down, what can I do
It's hard to stay one step ahead of you

One step ahead of you
Time is running out
Catching up with you

One step ahead of you
When I hold you close
Can I really lose?
One step ahead
Only one step ahead
She's one step ahead of you

SHIPS

N. FINN

Even ships of the night
Send out the alarm
My face is turning white
In case of emergency
I wonder if I might, slow down rest up

I'd like to get away
If my doctor lets me
Here in my waiting room
I'm pacing nervously
But I'm no give-away
Deep down messed up
Hit town dressed up
To the nines, to the nines, to the nines, to the nines

Some people pop a pill, when they feel exposed
Long as I'm dressed to kill
I'll make sure no-one knows
Disguised in fancy-dress
Deep down, messed up
Hit town dressed up
To the nines, to the nines, to the nines, my disguise

TRUE COLOURS

I GOT YOU

N. FINN

I got you—that's all I want
I won't forget—that's a whole lot
I don't go out—not now that you're in
Sometimes we shout—but that's no problem

I don't know why sometimes I get frightened
You can see my eyes, you can tell that I'm not lyin'

Look at you—you're a pageant
You're everything—that I've imagined
Something's wrong—I feel uneasy
Reassure me—tell me you're not teasin'

I don't know why sometimes I get frightened
You can see my eyes, you can tell that I'm not lyin'
I don't know why sometimes I get frightened
You can see my eyes, can you tell me you're not lyin'

There's no doubt—not when I'm with you
When I'm without—I stay in my room
Where do you go—I get no answer
You're always out—it gets on my nerves

I don't know why sometimes I get frightened
You can see my eyes, you can tell that I'm not lying
(But) I don't know why sometimes I get frightened
You can see my eyes, can you tell me you're not lyin'
I don't know why sometimes I get frightened
You can see my eyes, you can tell that I'm not lying

MISSING PERSON

N. FINN

Home too sweet home, it just occurred to me
To be on my own, in search of bitter treats
I get so removed but you never notice it
Step in my shoes, you'll see that I don't fit

I walk home, the wrong way, hoping I'll go astray
I'd like to be a missing person

Eyes open wide, but all I see is black
You thought I was all right just wait 'til you get back
There'll be no-one home
And they'll stay up all night
Everyone I know, I'm wishing you goodnight

I walk home, the wrong way, hoping I'll go astray
I'd like to be a missing person
I wander the highways, asleep in your doorways
I'm wanted but I'm a missing person

Missing Person

And I fly by night, fighting to get away
On the neon lights I slip down alley ways
Only safe and sound when silence brings a chill
Now my back is turned, I know I can't stand still

I walk home the wrong way, this time I'll go astray
I like to be a missing person
I wander the highways, asleep in your doorways
I'm wanted but I'm a missing person

Missing person, missing person, missing person ...

WHAT'S THE MATTER WITH YOU?
N. FINN

What's the matter with you?
Look down on everything we do
I really wonder if you see today like I do
What's the matter with you?

What's the matter with you?
You don't look cool in shades of blue
I really wonder if you see today like I do
What's the matter with you?

When I got up today I felt so much brighter
My head was swimming with delight and I told her
But she said 'What's so good about today?'
And she walked away
She's down in the dumps without a reason why

What's the matter with you?
Look down on everything we do
I really wonder if you see today like I do
What's the matter with you?

Gonna keep an eye on you, I'll be your dictator
So you better buck up or I'll deal with you later
So beat the drum and let the trumpet blow
You gotta let go
In the heat of the moment you reap what you sow

What's the matter with you?
Look down on everything we do
I really wonder if you see today like I do
What's the matter with you?

The worried look that's on your face makes you older
You realise that things have never been better
Yes sir, the weather's clear
There's Eskimos, in summer clothes
I don't suppose you'd like to laugh with me

What's the matter with you?
You look down on everything we do
I really wonder if you see today like I do
What's the matter with you?

MISCELLANEOUS

Mary Of The South Seas

N. FINN / T. FINN / A. WHITE

She boarded the boat a long time ago
It opened her up to the world
But time goes so slowly
You won't see it pass
A phone call from Dublin I'm with you at last

And I swear that I've always worked hard to be good
Just like I promised you once
And if I could spare you
You know that I would
Strange things can happen in this heat

Mary of the South Seas
Mary of the South
Mary of the South Seas
I feel your presence
Do you remember me

The sea is so swollen it's golden and silver
And all is a beckoning wave
The beauty contestant
On a ship from Southampton
The stars look so different from here

Mary of the South Seas
Mary of the South
Mary of the South Seas
I feel your presence
Do you remember me

I wish I could help you, it's hard to discover
The ones that you love slip away
So go on your journey
And when you recover
All the dreams that you've buried
Shall bloom in the day

Mary of the South Seas
Mary of the South
Mary of the South Seas
I feel your presence
Do you remember me

DOTS ON THE SHELLS

N. FINN / M. YUNUPINGU

Yarryarryurru gunbilk marrawuwul
Djambi dhuru warrpititi
Dhawalnydja dhuwala marrawurrtjara
Dhawalnydja dhuwala dhuruthuruya

And the lines on your face
The answer is there
And the light in your eyes
Don't hide it away
Like the dots on the shells
They shine

Dhawalanydja dhuwala dirrmalaya
Dhawalanydja dhuwala lunjgurrmaya
Ya wo ya wo ganyawuya
Ya wo ya wo yangayana

And the lines on your face
The answer is here
And the light in your eyes
Don't hide it away
Like the dots on the shells
They shine

And water's edge does on
Always rolling into the horizon
We'll go down where the octopus plays
Changing colour with the incoming day

And the lines on your face
The answer is here
And the light in your eyes
Don't hide it away
Like the dots on the shells
They shine

Like the stars
In the sky tonight
Like the lights
In the city tonight

Spirit Of The Stairs

N. FINN

You see the truth and he cannot hide
You're so in tune, you feel it inside
Justice revenge, tickle all over
Lily and sword, damnation reward
The spirit of the stairs
What everyone thinks but no one dares
And wishes make a sad lament
After he's gone

Ridicule of envy you can't forget me
Cos I'm fixed in your mind like a knot in the twine
The spirit of the stairs
What everyone thinks but no one hears
And wishes make a sad lament
After he's gone
After he's gone to the dogs of pouring rain
Hear my wooden footsteps on her train
Hear my wooden footsteps again
Tough outer shell not so you can tell
He's soft underneath where you sink your teeth
The spirit of the stairs
What everyone thinks but no one dares
And wishes make a sad lament
After he's gone

Mischance, too bad you're tongue-tied
How many times a day too dumb, too shy
Two, three, four, five, count the stairs
Think about what I should've said
After he's gone

Index of Titles

Index of First Lines